Mike Nero
And The
Superhero School

Written by Natasha Melissa Carlow
Illustrated by Kyle Stephen

Purple Butterfly Press

An Imprint of Kat Biggie Press

Columbia, SC

Library of Congress Control Number: 2021911531
ISBN: 978-1-955119-02-3

Illustrations by Kyle Stephen
Design by Margaret Cogswell, margaretcogswell.com
Purple Butterfly Press, purplebutterflypress.net
Printed in the United States of America

PURPLE BUTTERFLY PRESS

purplebutterflypress.net

Publisher's Cataloging-In-Publication Data
(Prepared by The Donohue Group, Inc.)

Names: Carlow, Natasha Melissa, author. | Stephen, Kyle, illustrator.
Title: Mike Nero and the Superhero School / written by Natasha Melissa Carlow ; illustrated by Kyle Stephen.
Description: Columbia, SC : Purple Butterfly Press, an imprint of Kat Biggie Press, [2022] | Interest age level: 005-008. |
    Summary: "First days can be tough, especially for someone as shy as Mikey, but Mikey's new school is a little different. On his first day,
    he meets his principal and some incredible children who help him discover his own superpower within and he learns that no matter what
    we may look like on the outside, everyone has something that makes them valuable"-- Provided by
    publisher.
Identifiers: ISBN 9781955119023 (hardback) | ISBN 9781955119030 (paperback) | ISBN 9781955119047 (ebook)
Subjects: LCSH: Child superheroes--Juvenile fiction. | First day of school--Juvenile fiction. | Ability in children--Juvenile fiction. |
    Self-esteem in children--Juvenile fiction. | CYAC: Superheroes--Juvenile fiction. | First day of school--Juvenile fiction. | Ability--Juve-
    nile fiction. | Self-esteem--Juvenile fiction.
Classification: LCC PZ7.1.C399 Mi 2022 (print) | LCC PZ7.1.C399 (ebook) | DDC [E]--dc23

I DEDICATE THIS BOOK TO KINDNESS
and to the people who practice it.
People like my son Caspian, whose heart
and mind amaze and inspire me daily.

To Hyacinth, Kylelan, and Kyleigh of course.

And to Dr. Cherisse Rambarose who
helped make this book possible.

My name is Mike Nero and today I start a new school. Standing outside the school building this morning, I held Mommy and Daddy's hands tightly. What if this was like the last school? Would I make any new friends at all?

My new principal, Mr. Joseph, met us at the front door and smiled warmly.

"Hello Mikey. Shall we take a tour?"

We followed Mr. Joseph through the door and down the long corridor. As we walked we saw students hustling to get to their classrooms. Walking along the hall was a boy who was older than me. He wore big, dark shades and had a long stick that beeped as he moved from side to side.

"What is he doing?" I asked Mr. Joseph

"Why don't you ask him? James, can you come here for a minute?"

James turned his head in our direction and smiled.

"Sure thing Mr. J," James said coming straight over to us moving his stick left and right on the floor.

"Mikey, this is James. Would you like to say hello?"

"Hello, James. I'm Mikey," I replied shyly.

"Mikey was just wondering what you were doing with your stick," said Mr. Joseph.

"I'm blind. That means that my eyes don't work so I have to use this cane to make sure that I don't bump into anyone or anything.

"What I do is move my cane back and forth gently across the floor, so that if I feel anything in the path of the cane, I know to move out of the way. So the cane kinda sees for me. Understand?" James asked kindly.

"I do, but if you can't see, how did you know where we were just now? You walked right over to us!"

"That's the best part. Even though my eyes don't work, I can hear sounds really well and I'm good at locating those sounds. So when Mr. J called my name I was able to tell which direction he was standing and follow the sound."

"Whoa, that's amazing!"

"Yep, it's pretty cool. Anyway, if you need anything at all, feel free to ask, okay? Don't be a stranger!"

"Wow, Daddy did you hear that? James is so cool!"

"He sure is, son," Daddy responded with a laugh.

We followed Mr. Joseph through the school, and he pointed out the library and lunchroom. A few students were eating in the lunch room, when they saw Mr. Joseph, they waved their hands excitedly.

Mr. Joseph waved back and began moving his fingers. Then, the kids at the table started moving their fingers too!

"What are they doing?" I asked reaching for Mommy's hand.

"Oh honey, I think these children are all deaf. They are using sign language," Mommy replied.

Mr. Joseph turned back to us and said: "That's right Mikey, would you like to say hi to them?"

"Umm okay." I shrugged.

"I want you to touch your hand to your head as if giving a salute and then bring it forward like this."

I put my hand to my head like I was a soldier, then moved my hand forward. The kids threw their hands in the air and moved their wrists back and forth.

"That means you did a good job, Mikey. They are giving you a round of applause!"

"Awesome. Wait so being deaf means you can't hear, right?"

"That's right."

"Does it mean you can't speak, too?"

"That's a great question!" one of the students said walking over to us.

"It is true that some people who are deaf can't speak, but that's not true for everyone. Sometimes, *deaf* people can speak like me but their hearing just isn't the same, so we use these hearing aids." She pulled her hair back and pointed to two little things attached to her ears.

"And sometimes *deaf* people can't hear or speak at all. So using sign language or talking with our hands gives us the ability to communicate with other people. We can even be in a room full of people and send secret messages to each other from across the room," she said with a wink. "But we also love helping the students who can hear just fine learn to use sign language."

"That's awesome. It's like you speak a secret language. Can you teach me your secret language?" Sometimes people have trouble understanding me when I speak so maybe if I learned this secret language too it would be easier.

"I sure will," she replied. "I am Stacy. I think we may be in the same class. Our teacher told us we were getting a new classmate this week!"

"Nice to meet you!" I replied excitedly, grinning at mommy and daddy as Stacy waved goodbye.

Touching me on my shoulder Mr. Joseph asked, "How are you doing there Mikey? Is walking too much for you? I want to show you the playground, but I know it can be tough for you-"

He was interrupted by a little girl in front of us who was standing in the corner of the hall covering her ears with her hands and shaking her head from side to side.

She seemed very upset and her teacher was kneeling in front of her speaking to her in a calm, soothing voice and offering her a pair of headphones.

"What happened to her?" I whispered to Mr. Joseph, feeling very concerned for her. "That's Amy. She is an awesome little girl. Would you like to meet her?"

"I don't know, I don't want to upset her," I replied.

"Why don't we check in on her for a bit and see?"

"Hello, Amy is everything alright?" Mr. Joseph asked kindly.

"I'm okay, I just didn't like the noise," Amy replied.

"Ah, I understand. I'll be sure to remind the other students to keep it down."

"Thank you," Amy replied, removing her headphones slowly.

"Amy this is Mikey, he's a new student here and he wanted to make sure that you were okay," Mr. Joseph said.

"Hello Mikey," Amy said, "I'm okay, sometimes with my autism, I can't always handle loud noises and the boys were pretending to drum so I needed to get away from all the noise," Amy explained.

"Oh, I'm sorry," I said. "Sometimes loud noises really bother me too."

"It's okay, I can use the headphones to help drown out the extra noise, you want to see the puzzle I'm building?" Amy asked cheerfully.

"Sure!" I replied following her to her classroom.

Sometime later, we followed Mr. Joseph out of the building to the playground area. Kids were playing on the swing sets, monkey bars, and jumping over hurdles. At the door, I stopped and looked at my parents. Mommy knelt beside me and asked, "What's up, son?"

"It's just that everyone here is so cool. They all have these great su-perpowers. James has a magic cane, and Stacey and her friends have a secret language, and Amy is so smart, she is building a 2000 piece puzzle. And these other kids can run and swing and jump so well. I don't have any of that. Plus, I walk and talk funny. What if the kids all make fun of my Cerebral Palsy here too?" I cried.

"Oh, son," Mommy and Daddy put their arms around me.

Just then, two boys ran up to us.

"Hey, how come you are crying? Do you need any help?" one of them asked.

"You want to come play on the jungle gym with us?" the other boy offered.

"I want to but I can't because I have Cerebral Palsy and my muscles can't support me on the jungle gym," I responded nervously, wiping the tears away.

"Oh, I understand. I have Attention Deficit-Hyperactivity Disorder or ADHD, which means I can't always focus on what I am doing but my Mom gave me this squeeze ball and it helps," the first boy replied.

The second boy piped in, "You don't have to feel sad. I am really good at helping my friends. We can play another game. We just want to play with you. Do you know any good games to play? We can ask those kids over there if they want to play too."

"Sure. Have you ever played Pirate King? I can teach you," I said.

As the boys ran off to round up all the kids on the playground, Mr. Joseph touched me gently on the shoulder.

"Can I tell you something about this school? You see this isn't a regular school. This is a superhero school. So yes, every student here has a special superpower. Whether it's the students who ride in wheelchairs instead of walking, or those with special ways of communicating or thinking, or even those like Marcus and David, who can walk and talk without any challenges, they are all pretty amazing. But do you know why this school is so special? It's because every student here uses their talents and abilities to help each other out. Regardless of how we look on the outside. That's what makes us superheroes."

"And do you know what, Mikey?"

I stared at him in wonder.

"You have the greatest superpower of all — kindness. The ability to see the best in others and to make other people feel loved and included."

"Now, Mikey, I want you to be a superhero and use those powers to make as many friends as you can and to help everyone that you can and I promise you, you will realize that no matter what difficulties we may have—those we can see or those we can't see—we are all trying to do our best. Even me."

Mr. Joseph raised his pant leg. Instead of a regular leg, there was a shiny, metal leg. Mr. Joseph had a bionic leg! Just like Captain Courageous from my favorite cartoon!

"Whoa, that's so cool!" I cried out.

"Yeah, it is pretty cool Mikey, and so are you. You are my very own superhero and I am trusting you to be a good example to all your fellow students here."

Nodding my head bravely, I said goodbye to my parents and Mr. Joseph and walked over to join the group of students who were waving me over excitedly. I looked around at all my new schoolmates. It was time to get to work making some new friends.

THE
END

Cerebral Palsy is commonly referred to as CP and it is the name for disorders that affects how a person moves or maintains balance and posture.

There are different types of CP and not every diagnosis is the same. For e.g. some people with CP may not be able to walk or talk and others, like Mikey, may be able to walk with the assistance of special equipment like his cane.

CP is the most common motor disability in childhood and occurs because of abnormal brain development or damage to the brain early in its development.

Many children with CP are able to attend school and excel. Like all children, they require kindness, understanding, friendship and fun.

https://www.cdc.gov/ncbddd/cp/index.html

Mike Nero And The Superhero School: Discussion Questions

✳ Have you ever met someone who looked/walked or talked differently than you?

✳ Tell me about a time when you were brave and made a new friend?

✳ How would you want others to treat you if they thought you were different?

✳ We all have superpowers, how do you think you can use yours to make your school a better place?

✳ Do you think that on the inside, we are more different or alike?

We are *all* SUPERHEROES.